EMMANUEL JOSEPH

The Social Innovator, Psychology, Ethics, and Cultural Awareness in Modern Entrepreneurship

Copyright © 2025 by Emmanuel Joseph

All rights reserved. No part of this publication may be reproduced, stored or transmitted in any form or by any means, electronic, mechanical, photocopying, recording, scanning, or otherwise without written permission from the publisher. It is illegal to copy this book, post it to a website, or distribute it by any other means without permission.

First edition

This book was professionally typeset on Reedsy. Find out more at reedsy.com

Contents

1 Chapter 1: The Birth of a Social Innovator — 1
2 Chapter 2: The Psychological Landscape of Social Innovation — 3
3 Chapter 3: Ethical Foundations of Social Entrepreneurship — 5
4 Chapter 4: Cultural Awareness and Sensitivity in Social... — 7
5 Chapter 5: Building Inclusive Business Models — 9
6 Chapter 6: Navigating Ethical Challenges — 11
7 Chapter 7: Leveraging Technology for Social Impact — 13
8 Chapter 8: The Role of Partnerships and Collaboration — 15
9 Chapter 9: The Impact of Social Capital — 17
10 Chapter 10: Measuring and Evaluating Impact — 19
11 Chapter 11: Scaling Social Innovations — 21
12 Chapter 12: Sustaining Social Innovations — 23
13 Chapter 13: The Role of Mentorship in Social Innovation — 25
14 Chapter 14: The Power of Storytelling in Social Innovation — 27
15 Chapter 15: Advocacy and Policy Influence — 29
16 Chapter 16: The Future of Social Innovation — 31
17 Chapter 17: Reflections and Lessons Learned — 33

1

Chapter 1: The Birth of a Social Innovator

In the dynamic world of modern entrepreneurship, the emergence of the social innovator marks a significant shift towards a more conscientious and holistic approach to business. Unlike traditional entrepreneurs driven primarily by profit, social innovators seek to address societal issues through innovative solutions, balancing financial success with social impact. This chapter explores the foundational traits and motivations that define a social innovator, setting the stage for the intricate interplay of psychology, ethics, and cultural awareness that follows.

At the core of every social innovator lies a deep-seated empathy and a genuine desire to create positive change. This intrinsic motivation often stems from personal experiences, a heightened sense of social responsibility, or a profound awareness of systemic inequalities. Social innovators are characterized by their ability to identify unmet needs within their communities and envision creative solutions that challenge the status quo. Their journey begins with a strong sense of purpose, driving them to venture beyond conventional business practices and pursue ventures that align with their ethical values.

The psychology of social innovators is marked by a unique blend of resilience, adaptability, and visionary thinking. They possess the courage to navigate uncharted territories, embracing uncertainty and risk with a growth mindset. Social innovators are adept at leveraging their emotional intelligence to build strong relationships, inspire collaboration, and foster a sense of shared purpose among stakeholders. Their capacity to empathize with diverse perspectives enables them to create inclusive solutions that resonate with a wide range of individuals and communities.

Ethics play a pivotal role in shaping the decisions and actions of social innovators. Guided by principles of fairness, transparency, and accountability, they strive to create ventures that prioritize the well-being of people and the planet. Ethical considerations are woven into the fabric of their business models, influencing everything from supply chain practices to employee relations and environmental sustainability. This commitment to ethical integrity not only strengthens their credibility but also builds trust and loyalty among their supporters and customers.

2

Chapter 2: The Psychological Landscape of Social Innovation

The realm of social innovation is not just a professional endeavor but a psychological journey that demands a profound understanding of human behavior and motivation. Social innovators must delve into the intricacies of human psychology to design solutions that effectively address complex social challenges. This chapter delves into the psychological dimensions that underpin social innovation, shedding light on the cognitive processes, emotional intelligence, and behavioral insights that drive impactful change.

At the heart of social innovation lies a deep understanding of cognitive empathy, which allows innovators to grasp the thoughts and feelings of those they aim to help. By putting themselves in the shoes of their beneficiaries, social innovators can uncover the root causes of societal issues and design interventions that resonate on a personal level. This empathetic approach enables them to create solutions that are not only practical but also emotionally compelling, fostering a sense of connection and empowerment among the people they serve.

Emotional intelligence is a cornerstone of successful social innovation, enabling innovators to navigate the complexities of human relationships and dynamics. Social innovators must possess the ability to manage their own emotions and respond to the emotions of others with sensitivity and compassion. This emotional acuity allows them to build trust, resolve conflicts, and inspire collaboration among diverse stakeholders. By fostering an environment of psychological safety, social innovators can harness the collective intelligence and creativity of their teams, driving the co-creation of innovative solutions.

Behavioral insights are instrumental in designing effective social interventions that drive lasting change. Social innovators must be adept at understanding the behavioral patterns and decision-making processes of their target populations. By leveraging principles of behavioral economics and social psychology, they can design interventions that nudge individuals towards positive behaviors and outcomes. This could involve using incentives, social norms, or persuasive communication to encourage sustainable practices, healthy behaviors, or equitable access to resources.

3

Chapter 3: Ethical Foundations of Social Entrepreneurship

In the realm of social entrepreneurship, ethics form the bedrock upon which sustainable and impactful ventures are built. Social innovators are guided by a set of ethical principles that shape their decision-making, business practices, and interactions with stakeholders. This chapter explores the ethical foundations that underpin social entrepreneurship, highlighting the importance of integrity, accountability, and social justice in driving positive change.

Integrity is a fundamental value that defines the character and credibility of a social innovator. It encompasses honesty, transparency, and consistency in actions and decisions. Social innovators must uphold the highest standards of ethical conduct, ensuring that their ventures are built on a foundation of trust and respect. This involves being truthful in their communications, honoring commitments, and maintaining transparency in their operations. By embodying integrity, social innovators build strong relationships with their stakeholders and earn the trust and loyalty of their supporters.

Accountability is another critical aspect of ethical social entrepreneurship. Social innovators must take responsibility for the impact of their actions and decisions on people and the planet. This involves being accountable to their beneficiaries, customers, employees, and the broader community. Social innovators should establish mechanisms for monitoring and evaluating the social and environmental outcomes of their ventures, ensuring that they are making a positive difference. By embracing accountability, social innovators demonstrate their commitment to continuous improvement and responsible business practices.

Social justice is a driving force behind the work of many social innovators. They are motivated by a deep sense of fairness and a desire to address systemic inequalities and injustices. Social innovators seek to create ventures that promote equity, inclusion, and access to opportunities for marginalized and underserved populations. This involves challenging discriminatory practices, advocating for the rights and dignity of all individuals, and designing solutions that prioritize the well-being of vulnerable communities. By championing social justice, social innovators contribute to building a more just and equitable society.

4

Chapter 4: Cultural Awareness and Sensitivity in Social Innovation

Cultural awareness and sensitivity are essential components of effective social innovation. Social innovators must navigate diverse cultural contexts and understand the unique needs, values, and traditions of the communities they serve. This chapter explores the importance of cultural awareness in social innovation, highlighting the need for cultural competence, humility, and inclusivity in designing impactful solutions.

Cultural competence involves a deep understanding and appreciation of different cultures and their perspectives. Social innovators must be knowledgeable about the cultural backgrounds, beliefs, and practices of their target populations. This cultural awareness enables them to design solutions that are culturally relevant and respectful, fostering a sense of belonging and trust among the communities they serve. Social innovators should engage in continuous learning and self-reflection to enhance their cultural competence and avoid cultural biases or stereotypes.

Humility is a key virtue for social innovators working in diverse cultural contexts. It involves recognizing the limitations of one's own knowledge and being open to learning from others. Social innovators must approach their work with humility, acknowledging the wisdom and expertise of the communities they aim to help. This requires active listening, genuine collaboration, and a willingness to adapt their approaches based on the input and feedback of community members. By embracing humility, social innovators can build authentic and respectful relationships that drive co-creation and empowerment.

Inclusivity is a guiding principle for social innovators committed to cultural sensitivity. It involves creating spaces and opportunities for diverse voices to be heard and valued. Social innovators should prioritize the inclusion of marginalized and underrepresented groups in the design and implementation of their solutions. This could involve engaging in participatory decision-making, ensuring equitable access to resources, and addressing power imbalances that hinder meaningful participation. By fostering inclusivity, social innovators create ventures that reflect the diversity and richness of the communities they serve.

5

Chapter 5: Building Inclusive Business Models

Inclusive business models are essential for ensuring that social innovation benefits a wide range of stakeholders, including marginalized and underserved populations. This chapter explores the principles and strategies for designing inclusive business models that promote equity, access, and participation.

At the heart of inclusive business models lies a commitment to equitable access to opportunities and resources. Social innovators must design their ventures in a way that ensures fair treatment and equal access for all individuals, regardless of their socioeconomic status, race, gender, or other factors. This involves removing barriers to entry, providing affordable products and services, and creating pathways for upward mobility. By prioritizing inclusivity, social innovators can create ventures that contribute to a more just and equitable society.

Participation is another key principle of inclusive business models. Social innovators should engage their beneficiaries and stakeholders in the decision-making process, ensuring that their voices are heard and valued. This involves creating spaces for dialogue, collaboration, and co-creation, where diverse perspectives can be integrated into the design and implementation of solutions. By fostering a participatory approach, social innovators can build ventures that reflect the needs and aspirations of the communities they serve.

Cultural sensitivity is essential for designing inclusive business models that resonate with diverse populations. Social innovators must understand and respect the cultural values, beliefs, and practices of their target communities. This involves tailoring their products, services, and marketing strategies to align with cultural norms and preferences. By embracing cultural sensitivity, social innovators can create ventures that build trust and connection with their beneficiaries, fostering long-term relationships and impact.

6

Chapter 6: Navigating Ethical Challenges

Social innovators often face complex ethical challenges in their work, requiring them to navigate difficult decisions and dilemmas. This chapter explores common ethical challenges in social innovation and provides strategies for addressing them with integrity and transparency.

One of the most pressing ethical challenges in social innovation is balancing the pursuit of profit with social impact. Social innovators must ensure that their ventures are financially sustainable while prioritizing the well-being of their beneficiaries. This involves making difficult decisions about resource allocation, pricing, and investment. Social innovators should establish clear ethical guidelines and decision-making frameworks to navigate these challenges, ensuring that their actions align with their values and mission.

Transparency is another critical aspect of ethical social innovation. Social innovators must be open and honest about their operations, impact, and challenges. This involves sharing information with stakeholders, providing regular updates, and being accountable for their actions. Transparency builds trust and credibility, fostering strong relationships with beneficiaries, customers, and supporters. Social innovators should embrace transparency as a core value, ensuring that their ventures operate with integrity and openness.

Addressing power imbalances is a key ethical challenge in social innovation. Social innovators must recognize and address the power dynamics that exist within their ventures and communities. This involves creating equitable opportunities for participation, ensuring that marginalized voices are heard, and addressing systemic inequalities. Social innovators should establish mechanisms for feedback, advocacy, and empowerment, promoting social justice and equity in their work.

7

Chapter 7: Leveraging Technology for Social Impact

Technology plays a pivotal role in driving social innovation and creating scalable solutions to complex societal challenges. This chapter explores the ways in which social innovators can leverage technology to enhance their impact and reach.

Digital platforms offer social innovators the opportunity to connect with beneficiaries, stakeholders, and supporters on a global scale. Social innovators can use social media, websites, and mobile apps to disseminate information, engage with communities, and mobilize resources. These platforms enable social innovators to reach a wider audience, build awareness, and foster collaboration. By leveraging digital technology, social innovators can amplify their impact and drive meaningful change.

Data analytics is another powerful tool for social innovators, enabling them to gather insights, measure impact, and make informed decisions. Social innovators can use data to understand the needs and behaviors of their beneficiaries, track progress, and evaluate outcomes. This involves collecting and analyzing quantitative and qualitative data, using tools such as surveys, interviews, and analytics software. By harnessing the power of data, social innovators can optimize their solutions, improve efficiency, and achieve greater impact.

Emerging technologies such as artificial intelligence, blockchain, and the Internet of Things offer innovative opportunities for social impact. Social innovators can explore the potential of these technologies to address complex societal challenges, such as poverty, healthcare, and environmental sustainability. This involves staying informed about technological advancements, collaborating with tech experts, and experimenting with new solutions. By embracing emerging technologies, social innovators can drive transformative change and create a better future.

8

Chapter 8: The Role of Partnerships and Collaboration

Partnerships and collaboration are essential for driving social innovation and achieving sustainable impact. This chapter explores the importance of building strong relationships with diverse stakeholders, including nonprofits, governments, businesses, and communities.

Nonprofit organizations are valuable partners for social innovators, offering expertise, resources, and networks to support their ventures. Social innovators can collaborate with nonprofits to co-create solutions, share knowledge, and mobilize resources. These partnerships enable social innovators to leverage the strengths and capabilities of nonprofits, driving collective impact and achieving common goals.

Government agencies play a crucial role in supporting social innovation through policy, funding, and regulation. Social innovators can engage with governments to advocate for supportive policies, access funding opportunities, and ensure compliance with regulations. These partnerships enable social innovators to scale their impact, influence systemic change, and contribute to the public good.

Businesses offer valuable resources and capabilities for social innovators, including funding, expertise, and market access. Social innovators can collaborate with businesses to create shared value, driving social and environmental impact alongside financial success. These partnerships enable social innovators to leverage the strengths and resources of the private sector, driving innovation and achieving sustainable outcomes.

Communities are the heart of social innovation, offering invaluable insights, support, and collaboration. Social innovators must engage with communities to understand their needs, build trust, and co-create solutions. These partnerships enable social innovators to foster meaningful relationships, drive community-led change, and achieve lasting impact.

9

Chapter 9: The Impact of Social Capital

Social capital is a crucial asset for social innovators, providing the networks, relationships, and trust needed to drive impactful change. This chapter explores the concept of social capital and its importance in social innovation, highlighting strategies for building and leveraging social capital to achieve sustainable outcomes.

Social capital is built on the foundation of trust, reciprocity, and mutual support. Social innovators must invest in building strong relationships with their stakeholders, including beneficiaries, partners, and supporters. This involves fostering open communication, demonstrating reliability, and showing genuine care for the well-being of others. By building trust, social innovators create a supportive network that can mobilize resources, share knowledge, and collaborate on solutions.

Reciprocity is another key aspect of social capital, involving the exchange of resources, support, and benefits among stakeholders. Social innovators should cultivate a culture of reciprocity, where individuals and organizations are encouraged to give and receive help. This could involve sharing expertise, providing mentorship, or offering financial support. By promoting reciprocity, social innovators create a collaborative ecosystem where everyone contributes to and benefits from collective efforts.

Mutual support is essential for sustaining social capital and driving long-term impact. Social innovators must prioritize the well-being of their stakeholders, providing support and assistance when needed. This could involve offering emotional support, advocating for the rights of beneficiaries, or addressing challenges faced by partners. By demonstrating mutual support, social innovators build strong, resilient networks that can withstand challenges and drive positive change.

10

Chapter 10: Measuring and Evaluating Impact

Measuring and evaluating impact is critical for social innovators to assess the effectiveness of their solutions, demonstrate accountability, and drive continuous improvement. This chapter explores the principles and methods for measuring and evaluating social impact, highlighting best practices and challenges.

Defining clear goals and objectives is the first step in measuring impact. Social innovators must establish specific, measurable, achievable, relevant, and time-bound (SMART) goals that reflect their mission and desired outcomes. This involves identifying key performance indicators (KPIs) that align with their objectives and tracking progress over time. By setting clear goals, social innovators can focus their efforts and measure the success of their interventions.

Data collection is essential for evaluating impact, providing the information needed to assess outcomes and make informed decisions. Social innovators should use a mix of quantitative and qualitative data collection methods, such as surveys, interviews, focus groups, and observation. This enables them to capture a comprehensive picture of their impact, considering both numerical data and personal experiences. By collecting reliable and relevant data, social innovators can evaluate the effectiveness of their solutions and identify areas for improvement.

Analysis and interpretation of data are critical for drawing meaningful insights and making evidence-based decisions. Social innovators should use statistical and qualitative analysis techniques to analyze their data, identifying trends, patterns, and correlations. This involves comparing actual outcomes with expected goals, assessing the factors that contributed to success or challenges, and making recommendations for future actions. By interpreting their data effectively, social innovators can drive continuous improvement and enhance their impact.

11

Chapter 11: Scaling Social Innovations

Scaling social innovations is a key goal for many social innovators, enabling them to expand their reach and amplify their impact. This chapter explores the strategies and challenges of scaling social innovations, highlighting best practices and examples.

Replication is a common strategy for scaling social innovations, involving the duplication of successful models in new locations or contexts. Social innovators should identify the core elements of their solutions that are essential for success and ensure that these elements are replicated consistently. This involves developing clear guidelines, training materials, and support systems to facilitate replication. By replicating successful models, social innovators can expand their reach and achieve greater impact.

Adaptation is another approach to scaling social innovations, involving the modification of solutions to suit different contexts or populations. Social innovators should assess the unique needs, preferences, and conditions of their target populations and adapt their solutions accordingly. This involves engaging with local stakeholders, conducting needs assessments, and iterating on solutions based on feedback. By adapting their innovations, social innovators can ensure that their solutions are relevant and effective in diverse contexts.

Partnerships and collaboration are essential for scaling social innovations, providing the resources, expertise, and networks needed for expansion.

Social innovators should build strong relationships with partners who can support their scaling efforts, including nonprofits, governments, businesses, and communities. This involves leveraging the strengths and capabilities of partners, sharing resources, and co-creating solutions. By fostering collaboration, social innovators can achieve greater impact and reach a wider audience.

12

Chapter 12: Sustaining Social Innovations

Sustainability is a critical aspect of social innovation, ensuring that solutions continue to create positive impact over the long term. This chapter explores the principles and strategies for sustaining social innovations, highlighting best practices and challenges.

Financial sustainability is essential for the long-term success of social innovations, providing the resources needed to continue operations and scale impact. Social innovators should develop diverse revenue streams, including grants, donations, earned income, and investments. This involves building strong relationships with funders, demonstrating impact, and developing sustainable business models. By ensuring financial sustainability, social innovators can maintain their operations and drive lasting change.

Organizational capacity is another key aspect of sustainability, involving the development of skills, knowledge, and systems to support long-term success. Social innovators should invest in building the capacity of their teams, providing training, mentorship, and professional development opportunities. This involves developing strong leadership, effective management practices, and robust operational systems. By building organizational capacity, social innovators can ensure that their ventures are resilient and capable of sustaining impact.

Community engagement is critical for sustaining social innovations, ensuring that solutions remain relevant and effective. Social innovators should prioritize ongoing engagement with their beneficiaries and stakeholders, seeking input, feedback, and collaboration. This involves building strong relationships, fostering trust, and creating opportunities for participation. By engaging with their communities, social innovators can ensure that their solutions continue to meet the needs and aspirations of the people they serve.

13

Chapter 13: The Role of Mentorship in Social Innovation

Mentorship is a powerful tool for social innovators, providing guidance, support, and inspiration. This chapter explores the importance of mentorship in social innovation, highlighting the benefits and strategies for finding and nurturing mentor relationships.

Mentors offer valuable insights and experience, helping social innovators navigate the challenges and opportunities of their journey. They provide guidance on strategic decision-making, offer feedback on ideas and plans, and share their own experiences and lessons learned. By leveraging the knowledge and expertise of mentors, social innovators can avoid common pitfalls, accelerate their growth, and achieve greater impact.

Support is another key benefit of mentorship, providing social innovators with emotional and practical assistance. Mentors offer encouragement, motivation, and a sounding board for ideas and concerns. They provide a safe space for social innovators to discuss their challenges and explore potential solutions. By receiving support from mentors, social innovators can build resilience and confidence, enabling them to persevere through difficulties and setbacks.

Finding the right mentor is essential for a successful mentorship relationship. Social innovators should seek mentors who share their values, vision, and commitment to social impact. This involves identifying potential mentors within their networks, attending industry events, and seeking recommendations from peers. Social innovators should approach potential mentors with a clear understanding of their goals and expectations, fostering a mutually beneficial relationship.

Nurturing mentorship relationships requires ongoing effort and communication. Social innovators should prioritize regular check-ins, express gratitude for their mentor's support, and actively seek their feedback and advice. This involves being open and transparent about their progress, challenges, and needs. By investing in their mentorship relationships, social innovators can build lasting connections that drive personal and professional growth.

14

Chapter 14: The Power of Storytelling in Social Innovation

Storytelling is a powerful tool for social innovators, enabling them to communicate their vision, inspire action, and build support. This chapter explores the role of storytelling in social innovation, highlighting the techniques and benefits of effective storytelling.

Compelling narratives are essential for engaging and inspiring stakeholders. Social innovators should craft stories that resonate with their audience, highlighting the human impact of their work. This involves sharing personal experiences, testimonials, and case studies that illustrate the real-world benefits of their solutions. By creating emotionally compelling narratives, social innovators can capture the hearts and minds of their audience, fostering empathy and support.

Clarity and simplicity are key principles of effective storytelling. Social innovators should communicate their vision and impact in a clear and concise manner, avoiding jargon and complexity. This involves distilling their message into a few key points that are easy to understand and remember. By simplifying their message, social innovators can ensure that their stories are accessible and relatable to a wide range of audiences.

Authenticity is another critical aspect of storytelling, involving the honest and genuine portrayal of experiences and impact. Social innovators should share their successes and challenges with transparency, highlighting the realities of their journey. This involves being vulnerable and open about their struggles, failures, and lessons learned. By embracing authenticity, social innovators can build trust and credibility with their audience, fostering deeper connections and support.

Visual and multimedia elements can enhance the impact of storytelling, providing a richer and more engaging experience. Social innovators can use photos, videos, infographics, and other visual tools to illustrate their stories and bring their work to life. This involves leveraging digital platforms and social media to share their stories with a broader audience. By incorporating visual and multimedia elements, social innovators can create more immersive and impactful narratives.

15

Chapter 15: Advocacy and Policy Influence

Advocacy and policy influence are essential components of social innovation, enabling social innovators to drive systemic change and address root causes of societal issues. This chapter explores the strategies and challenges of advocacy and policy influence, highlighting the role of social innovators in shaping public policy.

Advocacy involves raising awareness and mobilizing support for social issues and solutions. Social innovators should use their platforms and networks to amplify their message, engage stakeholders, and build coalitions. This involves leveraging media, social media, and public speaking opportunities to reach a wider audience. By engaging in advocacy, social innovators can build momentum and support for their cause, driving collective action and change.

Policy influence involves engaging with policymakers and government agencies to shape public policy and regulations. Social innovators should build relationships with key decision-makers, participate in policy forums, and provide evidence-based recommendations. This involves conducting research, collecting data, and presenting compelling arguments for policy change. By influencing policy, social innovators can create a more supportive environment for their work and drive systemic change.

Collaboration with advocacy organizations and coalitions can enhance the impact of social innovators' efforts. Social innovators should partner with organizations that share their goals and values, working together to advocate for policy change. This involves coordinating efforts, sharing resources, and leveraging each other's strengths. By collaborating with advocacy organizations, social innovators can amplify their voice and achieve greater impact.

Navigating the complexities of advocacy and policy influence requires strategic thinking and perseverance. Social innovators must be prepared to face resistance, navigate bureaucracy, and address competing interests. This involves developing a clear advocacy strategy, staying informed about policy developments, and being adaptable to changing circumstances. By remaining committed and strategic, social innovators can drive meaningful policy change and advance their mission.

16

Chapter 16: The Future of Social Innovation

The future of social innovation is shaped by emerging trends, challenges, and opportunities. This chapter explores the future landscape of social innovation, highlighting key trends and the potential for transformative impact.

Technological advancements are set to play a significant role in the future of social innovation. Emerging technologies such as artificial intelligence, blockchain, and renewable energy offer new possibilities for addressing complex societal challenges. Social innovators should stay informed about technological developments, explore innovative applications, and leverage technology to enhance their impact. By embracing technology, social innovators can drive transformative change and create a more sustainable and equitable future.

Climate change and environmental sustainability are pressing issues that will continue to shape the future of social innovation. Social innovators must prioritize sustainability in their solutions, addressing the environmental impact of their ventures and promoting sustainable practices. This involves developing green technologies, advocating for environmental policies, and raising awareness about climate change. By focusing on sustainability, social innovators can contribute to a more resilient and sustainable world.

Social equity and inclusion will remain critical priorities for social innovation. Social innovators must address systemic inequalities and ensure that their solutions promote equity and inclusion for all individuals. This involves challenging discriminatory practices, advocating for marginalized communities, and designing inclusive solutions. By prioritizing social equity, social innovators can create a more just and equitable society.

Global collaboration and partnerships will be essential for addressing complex global challenges. Social innovators must build strong relationships with international organizations, governments, and communities, fostering collaboration and knowledge-sharing. This involves participating in global forums, engaging in cross-cultural dialogue, and leveraging global networks. By fostering global collaboration, social innovators can drive collective action and achieve greater impact.

17

Chapter 17: Reflections and Lessons Learned

The journey of a social innovator is marked by continuous learning, reflection, and growth. This final chapter reflects on the key lessons learned and offers insights for aspiring social innovators.

Resilience and perseverance are essential qualities for social innovators, enabling them to navigate challenges and setbacks. Social innovators must embrace a growth mindset, viewing failures as opportunities for learning and improvement. This involves staying committed to their vision, remaining adaptable to changing circumstances, and seeking support from mentors and peers. By cultivating resilience, social innovators can overcome obstacles and drive lasting impact.

Collaboration and community engagement are critical for the success of social innovation. Social innovators must prioritize building strong relationships with their stakeholders, fostering trust, and creating opportunities for participation. This involves actively listening to the needs and perspectives of their communities, co-creating solutions, and promoting mutual support. By fostering collaboration, social innovators can achieve collective impact and drive meaningful change.

Ethics and integrity are the cornerstones of social innovation, guiding decisions and actions. Social innovators must uphold the highest standards of ethical conduct, ensuring that their ventures prioritize the well-being of people and the planet. This involves being transparent, accountable, and committed to social justice. By embodying ethics and integrity, social innovators can build trust, credibility, and lasting impact.

Continuous learning and reflection are essential for personal and professional growth. Social innovators must seek opportunities for learning, stay informed about emerging trends, and reflect on their experiences. This involves engaging in lifelong learning, seeking feedback, and embracing a mindset of curiosity and exploration. By prioritizing continuous learning, social innovators can enhance their skills, knowledge, and impact.

The Social Innovator: Psychology, Ethics, and Cultural Awareness in Modern Entrepreneurship

In "The Social Innovator: Psychology, Ethics, and Cultural Awareness in Modern Entrepreneurship," we journey through the intricacies of a new wave of entrepreneurship that prioritizes social impact alongside financial success. This book delves into the essential traits and motivations that drive social innovators, balancing empathy, resilience, and visionary thinking.

We explore the deep psychological landscape that underpins social innovation, focusing on cognitive empathy, emotional intelligence, and behavioral insights. Ethical foundations are examined thoroughly, highlighting the principles of integrity, accountability, and social justice that guide social innovators.

Cultural awareness and sensitivity emerge as critical components in designing inclusive business models. This book emphasizes the importance of understanding diverse cultural contexts and engaging communities with humility and inclusivity.

Technology's role in amplifying social impact is discussed, showcasing how digital platforms, data analytics, and emerging technologies like AI and blockchain can drive transformative change. Partnerships and collaboration are underscored as essential for achieving sustainable impact, with insights into building relationships with nonprofits, governments, businesses, and communities.

We also delve into the crucial aspects of measuring and evaluating impact,

CHAPTER 17: REFLECTIONS AND LESSONS LEARNED

scaling social innovations, and ensuring sustainability. The significance of mentorship, storytelling, advocacy, and policy influence is explored, providing practical strategies for aspiring social innovators.

Looking ahead, the book contemplates the future of social innovation, with a focus on technological advancements, climate change, social equity, and global collaboration. Finally, reflections and lessons learned offer valuable insights for those embarking on their journey as social innovators.

www.ingramcontent.com/pod-product-compliance
Lightning Source LLC
LaVergne TN
LVHW020459080526
838202LV00057B/6053